THE LAST THING STANDING

THE LAST THING STANDING

Ann Shin

The Mansfield Press

Canadian Cataloguing in Publication Data

Shin, Ann
the last thing standing

Poems
ISBN 1-894469-03-8

1. Title

PS8587.H4786L37 2000 C811'.6 C00-930571-8

The author would like to acknowledge the
generous support of the Canada Council
and would like to thank Margaret Christakos
and especially Diana Fitzgerald Bryden
for their support and editorial suggestions.

Some of these poems first appeared in
Geography of Encounters (Roman and Little Press),
Crossroads Cant (Broken Jaw Press),
Shift, *Canadian Forum* and *Fireweed*.

Cover design by Bryan Gee
Cover photo by Dennis Lago
Text design in FF Scala by Colin Christie
Author photo page 58 by Jackie Newstadt

The **Mansfield** Press
25 MANSFIELD AVENUE, TORONTO, ONTARIO, CANADA. M6J 2A9
Publisher: *Denis De Klerck*

This book is for Deni

THE LAST THING STANDING

DUSK

few places in a house rarely see the sun
dark corners where your soul is kept dry
coiled small as doors swing wide

opened and closed. a house to the wind
turns down its lights and awaits the fall of dusk
when souls growing large fill the breadth of a room
with rumours.

the bedroom smelling of sleep, tousled hair
the blue velour sofa bearing your body's handprint
musty clothes, old shoes and apples nestled
in the creaks of a house that owns you – others before you.

say you take down those walls, peel them down
like a fruit whose spine you can eat with your fingers,
what you find is not the residue of some memory
but that ellipsis in which all action's taken place

a moment: sitting on the living room floor
the 4 walls of your home fall away
like cards opening out in a hand that reveals
it's playing another game
and that is the real game,
not the house, not the body
but the motions you *go through going through the thing.*

laughing we peeled clementines and told stories in the dark
aunts, uncles, cousins all huddled faces glowing
farms snow-muffled but for a candle in the window
offering a secret handshake – *come, come in*
you are not lost. we are many in our homes, safe.
while past these lit roads, in the dark fields somewhere
between their homes and mine, the rest of the world's
lost.

thinking of that winter at my computer attempting
e-mail. it's me now, left out in the fields
watching darkness eat fenceposts, obliterate the sky.
no candles, no oranges, just a blank screen
and the mute expectation of logging on.

the slap of hand on hand abstracted into key clicks.
cool skin. dry skin. still bodies.
how far we've come

into this electric night,
one voice proliferates – my longing
for you, for hometown, for sagebrush and grasses –
is swallowed in the echo of the nameless.
this is the driest harvest, ourselves
in darkness.

stone walls and stairwells winding off in blue air
the mountain homes in Fikardou unbutton their blouses,
the sky takes its liberties.

giving most freely now their owners have left
pigeon droppings stain window stoops
in what used to be a courtyard where men met for drinks
as mom sipped her own in the kitchen.

bless this stone oven whose chimney
collapsed, has forgotten the smell of yeast
our mothers' hands have not shaped bread in years
nor harvested walnuts or the vines
splashing grapes onto the terraces.

at what point did they pick up and shrug
this is not worth it. a dropped
pitchfork handle bounces up and down as
surprised chickens flutter their flightless wings

there was a use for it once, but now
few live in the country.

a jeep engine fades down the sloping dirt road
as rain water sluices down half-eaten walls
dust rising and falling in ruins lived
and passed on. leave their hollowed rooms
leave them standing.

ENTRANCE

the front door like a hand with its palm facing in
barriers and beckons, promises opening.
come in to the inside, have a seat, here's some coffee.
you cross your legs getting comfortable breathing in
house smells – so begins the acquaintance.

or overdone to its extreme of tasseled curtains
and brass fittings, the front door as a mask
coat of arms, an arrangement of plastic flowers,
remains unopened. wanting familiarity
you saunter up the drive to stand
hesitating at the side screen door

while out back, the door flaps quietly.
returning from the yard
or stepping in from the garage, past laundry
to the steamy smell of leeks and stewed squash,
you place your hand on my back as you reach
for two glasses, and you're gone again
to the living room or the yard, I don't know
somewhere near.

RENOVATION

tearing down basement drywall
breathing clouds of gypsum and black dust
our dry lungs cough up bits of a house
we've begun cannibalizing.

clearing the sawdust behind ceiling boards my hand
knocks a girl's purse, her pink doll, her school photo
falls through the hole. I imagine
teasing laughter, kids scrambling up stairs.

this old house, drilled and prodded
as we make it into our own image
exposing heating ducts, wires
hanging from wooden joists –

how illusory, the finished surfaces of floors and walls,
and how comfortable the boxes in which we live our lives,
all hung on a skeleton of 2 by 4's,
we strip down the house to see huge pockets of air

the searing dry air of mediterranean hills
entering my lungs, blood quickens.

I've heard donkeys laden with grape leaves
clopping on stones with their hooves.
I walk with a stick made of cypress
and feel the weight settle in my knees.

earth crumbling under my fingers, rises
to my nostrils and ears, I hear
the slow note of harvest in long cornstalks
that give and give in the last breaths of summer.

I've memorized my grandmother's steps
and dance to her music
touch trees, pluck grapes
wish health to all villages.

and lying back in bed I hear the long note's decay.
our grandmothers pass on,
their shutters latched closed.
in their deaths the still world
is given to us.

leaves, branches
a trunk flowing with sap
sucked from the roots' soil below.
like resins in a tree place accrues in our bodies.
we know what the soil works within us

and we answer
to the trickle of cold night water
answer flowers who are closing their blooms
answer dogs who bark at the planes
that leave and arrive flying far from the stars
far from the earth below.

HALLWAYS

if rooms were the nouns of a dwelling
these are the prepositional phrases,
null spaces you pass through
on the road to the good stuff:
the bed, the TV, dinner, the tub.

the only time people linger in halls
is at parties where passageways
are coveted. you stand relishing your drink
as hair, hips, breasts suggest themselves,
quivers of

intimacy in the, at the, around the, by the
through and again, near.

pressing my lips against a glassed
promise of release, let me drink from afar
as the room's soft shuffling feet, scarves and perfume trail

behind me. I am somewhere between here
and your Jerusalem room's long sunlight
rippling strings of a grand piano
where I wish to lay my head.

play, for I am lost in a crowd
of muggy armpits, foul cigarettes
and a steel string is vibrating
with the last note's resonance

so I am listening to you
sitting down for the recital
your gas mask lying just off stage,
your fingers hit the keys
and I set my drink down
to steady myself.
if the threat of bombs can span a globe
then so does this love.

there is violence in the inhalation of breath
as air enters the body and pushes into its walls
it pummels a path toward the heart eagerly
as if it's never been done
each breath I take I fear invisible riots
roiling in the heavy atmosphere,
air pungent with the deaths of ancestors
urging me to their vendetta – *our lives*
were meant to have been better than this

how to breathe the air of our ancestors;
an action so common it seems negligible
but is as deliberate as a promise
or denial.

my mother and father
took their first breaths in a country I've never lived –
where she and her sister culled seaweed from the shore,
where his whole family worked together on open rice fields.

when I visit them now I take the subway to North York
and transfer to a bus, I know which one without looking
the distance between us become habitual, forgotten

but still,
when I step in their door
the heaviness in the lungs
the dense history within the rooms
which hold our bodies as we sit together

this heavy, warm air

balancing on a canoe touching fingertips
to keep from tipping, the water's surface
a sheer membrane we fall through, falling in,
the entire surface of our bodies swallowed
by a mouth cool and forgiving;
we stay there.

MORNING

the grapefruit peeling in seismic

disturbances, I don't know,
the peel falling plateward and fragrant

what this day will bring.
light falling across the table

as trees shift into more comfortable
standing positions.

the walls breathe supple psalms along the floors
to my feet

and in my hand a grapefruit lies
half-skinned

a wedge parting the screen door opens
and from the sunshine you walk in

we've divided the earth inside and out
and come up plenty.

the plant on my mantelpiece, I don't know its name
has sprouted a head of veiny green leaves
I turn over in bed and summer's
teeth are in me. souped up cars
tight tank tops, the world's a bustin'

a crushed mango, the day drips
down my cheeks, ripe strings of wet peach flesh
wind tunnels of warm leaves and petals
car horns, taxis, slow-moving
sweat salons.

I'll wade swamps and for once
feel alive in this city which has me
in its mandibles as I, mouth open
try to cram it in.

let the sidewalk slather me, I'm stepping out,
this is love at its giddiest, train tracking riskiest
odorific, wet slapping, muscle twitching grossest.
the city's pores have opened
and I'm sliding in.

elbow colliding into ribs, a spray of finely chopped onions
spatter the floor as a well placed thumb sprouts blood.
anger's heavy red face blooming between us, I swear
you'd grown 2 feet wider or stepped nimbly into
my path as we hit – now your thumb's
dripping all over the food.

rushed and pragmatic, I pull it to the kitchen sink
and mistakenly (I swear) turn on the hot water.
war. how deftly your other hand hucks eggs
at my chest. and oh, grated beets swiftly fly
until halted by your face. those red peppers
I spent 2 hours roasting and peeling – thank you they are
good for my skin. and for your hygiene I recommend
ricotta filled canelloni. whose idea was this dinner anyway?
okay it was my idea but this kitchen, now studded with sharps,
has become an island too small for the both of us. so jump.

BATHROOM

our moments of true privacy:

shit, phlegm, piss, plaque, hair,
dead skin, toenail clippings.

and this is love, this leggy sweat of our bodies in deep sleep
we wake in a blank room and the banter begins
between skilsaw and paint chips we fight tooth and nail
for what's really important, the agreement that abides
all disagreements, moving our limbs
as buried rivers stir divining rods
it quivers in our hands, pulls our bodies
humming toward that same compass point
home. returning we clash again
we argue, we tire, we sleep.

a kettle of sand carried across the fold
of my nightgown, my son is making tea
with backyard dirt and I am his
stove, my belly radiates red heat.
he's warming his fingers as he sits
on his bum, 10 toes pressing into me.

in turn my imagination takes us to sea
where the sun's spattered into millions
and we, sailless, catamaran our bodies
into lips through which water is sipped
by the sky weltering heat.

my small son, threshhold
for new identities, you are love
made clean. peach down shoulders
on the back of a father's daughter,
a grandma's smile
you are
new words between us.

fingers pressed together
you cradle the stone with both hands
rocking as it slowly
settles over the yellow kernels,
the grey stone worn smooth where
your palms each time
scoop the maize and pour
into the centre hole of the wheel stone.
grasping the wooden peg and pulling it around
you watch the maize sink as the stone slowly turns
without stopping you switch hands
your body swaying with each turn, as if keening
heel digging in as you lean into the wheel.

this is your meditation:
cracking the hard kernels
breaking them down
into a dusty pale powder.

a door slides open and he tumbles out to
crawl under your left arm and sit in your lap
as you continue your grinding, his chubby hands
make *phoosh phoosh* sounds in the bowl of cornflour.
you see the kernels, he sees the bread.

there is the memory of her breath, soft scrabbling
mice along the floorboards, my mother
washed the walls of that old house until
the stench was bearable. doors flung wide
as butterflies trussed their bedspreads outside
with the assurance of those who see order in chaos
weeds, long grasses, knuckles dirt-browned, ill-
served by thimbles I was never out of trouble.
my mother's books and bills neatly rolled
in elastic bands, her skinny legs and back like a
well worn chair with a rib cage that bowed
to fit it. I never caught a butterfly all the summers
we lived there, never tried enough, their wings too
frighteningly delicate I might crumple them in giant
clumsiness, quick fluttering death on my fingers.
orange, yellow, white petals in the air eddying
up in the evening sky my mother's breath
against my ear freed me into sleep. how luscious
the heat never oppressed and the field edged to my window
grasses swishing my bedroom carpet. slipping
headlong I slept like a riverbank receiving water
on its velvet clay chest. few words remembered, I don't pray anymore
but I garner moments attempting to understand how a heart
fills them in absence.

RECKONING

a lit bedroom at 3:00 in the morning is ungodly.
like cars at the scene of an accident time slows
and I'm neither casualty nor driver
I'm somewhere in the queue blinking
at the flare hot and high in the still air

my children's faces, my husband's arms

my soul standing crisp at attention, alone
has forgotten how it got here.
tomorrow will be dishes
a houseful of worries to pull me through
but until then, it's freefall

a jumble of furniture and duties

touching the walls of a dark hallway
I slump at my son's door to stare
at his curled body. I am a car
idling in a school parking lot
waiting for the bell to ring.

HOUSELOVE

I've poured years into it
this newly shingled, trim-painted
sand-blasted home. in my work room
sweatered, I hunch over a computer
cool air goosepimpling my leg hairs as
swooshes of autumn wind flap this
piece of quiet I'd just managed hoping
to settle down for the night but
for the life of me I can't get these windows
closed. rain conspires quietly against me
seeping into walls that stand erect, yes
but are beginning to bend elsewhere. my wayward
home, bastion of confidences for my
slow heart I pull this house over me
like a mothridden coat.

I thought I'd found solidity
but instead it's got me: caretaker
for its beastly needs. to the hammer ping
of radiators, the house shifts its girth
as the scales from my eyes, fall. rust
and broken beams betray your frailty
my crumbling heap of mortar and bricks,
my honey, my wooden locks,
my questionable love.

silhouettes of picture frames blemish the walls
like masks dismantled and stored in boxes
their cardboard flaps taped shut

the shelves, the sofas still in their proper places
but a few books missing, your mother's favourite vase
all her photographs that hung on the walls
her closet in the extra room, cleared empty.

winter upon your mother's dormant face.
her fatigue the kind a woman wears
when she has known something for too long

something splintered

your father's head in his hands
thinking and rethinking
what he can't put into words

and you
search for some moment of resolve
a birth of green
you search for your mother's eyes

recoil
collapse
into a small clenched fist

sorrow is incoherent

two people in a room emptied
of all its possessions
while the city snow slowly
covers everything

it's not so much a loss
as a willful closing down of space
memory curls in

I have a friend who shrinks the space she inhabits:
an empty room with one window
afternoon sun falls in
on nothing
on wooden floors.

she is steady as the beams which run through the walls.
when I hug her I am surprised
at the strength of her bones.

closed windows and doors, the rooms of her house
are filled with quiet chaos.
her calm like light
illuminating nothing,
she hovers

emotion
conjured from somewhere below
rises as a gust of hot air
rushes through her
and is gone.

I want to hold her and say everything
pluck objects from still air
to give the room furnishings –
soft-leaved plants, colour snapshots on the wall,
a winter sweater slung over a sitting chair,
I want to sit with her amongst her things
in the silence of doors left slightly ajar

I am finally
hollowed out.   clean.   bone dished
smooth, the wooden knife
scrapes along my breast bone.

an ache
draining through me
through the heels of my feet
has left a hollow

in my chest
where it's hard to breathe.
pierced. enlivened
as a glass of water is by light
as a room by a body's passing.

HOUSEWIFE'S TIP #3

the bare minimum:

your own entrance
a window
toilet paper

TO PICK

it starts as benign
concern for aesthetic,
you notice a chip on your nail
and pick at it, smooth it over
until there's just a thread a bit of nail
that grabs your fingertip as you rub it
you file it with another fingernail and it
peels away, pulling itself deeper into the nail.
this is not the way you want to go
but you watch it tear deeper into your finger.
the sliver hanging from your nail
there's no way you can leave it
so with two fingers you pull hard, feeling pain
the sliver tears and blood glistens. you suck
and go back to work noticing it hurts
when you grab a glass or pick up a pen.
at times it bleeds again.

white iron claw tub crouched fat on the tiles
I'm dripping soap suds and some good ol'
hair of the dog as afternoon sun screams in,
it's here we begin excavation

alone, naked, faucet running
there is little my hands control
as the spout before me
gushes. I am born

into a world before procreation
where passion – death even, is razed to this
minimal gesture, this planed angle
hinging backbone to legs.

at some point I swear these hips knew sex
these arms lifted crates of apples, but now
my limbs resting on chrome and white porcelain
aren't anything (awkwardly tendoned blue veins)

here, in the one room where I take it
all off, peel, scrub, exfoliate, wear away –
I come back to what's honest:
2 arms, 2 legs, a stretch of skin across the chest
and the will to go on with something I didn't start.

in the tub my body learns peace with the objects
remembers its roles in the world and submits,
the grainy iridescence of oatmeal soap on skin,
the stoop of my neck against the tub
most humbling.

MY MOTHER'S BACK

I used to scrub my mother's back
expansive and calm and warm, my mother

is as green as the leaves
blown dry by summer's evening wind.

my wish for her is days and days,
that a day will end
and another begin.

my mother enters memory
and waits in the wings

even as we speak
she waits in the wings

her throat savouring words
she's swallowed for too long

she is that youngest part of me
a fossil

pressed into igneous forms
folded in over years

to be discovered once hollowed,
I search for remains.

I recall washing her back
both bending forward

my hands on her skin, listening

the plunk of an apricot in a sinkful of water
wash your hands wash your hands
we are at table and waiting. late summer
confusion of relatives, farmers and too much fruit.
baskets of peaches left in garage corners
softly gather the aroma of sweet death and bruises.

plums dropping from trees like clothes we cast off
in the rush to get into new jeans.
I learned to carve apples from women whose time
peeled off in curls onto the floor.
mom's arms on the dining table as the knife
in her hand pulled heaps of skinned peaches
the days in her wheelchair drawn long and slow

we made preserves to get drunk by
nanny spilling rum over the jars, gulping
dribbly berries with her eyes tightly shut.
furtive with her drinks and embittered
by sons who've kicked her out –

how we crushed the berries
their skins tearing, juice spilling
as flesh strained out of itself leaving
purple red stains on our aprons – grisly birthing
aunts busily wiping jars worried
of late hours and husbands. we rushed
burning sugar, sweat and lipstick
rubbed into lip creases – cherry burst,
raspberry passion, peach blush, midnight
poisonberry. the mouth hoards its secrets
as hands crush. crush. crush.

winter is so heavy

of warmer climates and elephants
and graveyards, where did our memory

no
      no
don't go
the water has almost boiled
sit down for a bit. sit
it's been so long since I've seen you.

the cold, it is so cold.

(crocheted quilt on his lap)
I don't get the exercise I once did, or
just everything seems harder
you know what I mean
don't you

as if the sun were still setting

always picking up the paper
putting it down
shuffling from kitchen to sitting room
to kitchen
I can't see you love, where are you
I'm talking to you

I'm here   on the sofa

did
      you want some tea?

in sudden question, his eyes
(berries bursting in snow)

we almost speak

where are those papers
bent and searching
(not those slippers still)
the body is so familiar.

I keep missing it

crushing white daisies
against the bathrobe
his hand slowly sifts through the papers

those were for you

I know love, I know.

somewhere between the 3rd and 4th
butter'n jam toast I know I'm not hungry.
by my 6th it doesn't matter, I'm in neck deep
and my hands aren't responding, they're feeling
up candy wrappers, popcorn, jam danishes,
melting ice cream, toast in my mouth dribbling
drips of strawberry jam. I'm eating myself
into that comfortable sleeve one finds in food.
forehead sweaty and smooth as a beluga's belly,
I am sodden with limpid mortality. take me

I eat hard and fast so all things lose taste,
passion turns over in its skin and I am
covered by another numb, dumb skin.
suffocating, the tips of my fingers senseless,
toast crumbles onto the floor as I stop
(a silent kitchen)
when I start again I am alone
as before.

A HOUSE IS NOT THE ANSWER

I thought I'd find peace in 4 walls
wooden floors and a warm kitchen
with brown sugar in covered tins.

I thought the sun would be more pleasing
if I had a window that faced it
set with lace curtains and drapes.

I thought my love would untangle
with the curling laughter of kids
being tickled by two large hands.

I thought this grit would wash down
leaving drops of cool water
on glistening bathroom porcelain.

I scratch at my board of slate
and find nothing. nails, graphite,
shivers up my spine.

HOUSEWIFE'S TIP #5

squish it
into the sink.
force it down, squish it, mash it
shove it down the drain.
get rid of it get rid of it.

then get rid of the gloves.

morning fog thickening in my lungs, I trudged
with a coat over my nightgown and boots.
arms filled with prickly hay I approached them
crowding as eagerly as dogs to a door,
cows, their hooves slopping in manure
swinging their slow heads above my own
like clumsy masts in some mucked sea,
black eyes rolled wild in their sockets.

I feared their gaping eyes, feared
without reason, the way years fall slack
before you mid-step, you turn your head
and intention which had seemed noble enough
betrays itself.

this childhood fear never enters my dreams
but interrupts me in the middle of the day
at my desk, or looking up to cross a street
these beasts, their bland eyes stare back at me

eager mouths tugging hay from my arms
I drop my load and run back to let myself out of
the fenced field, I run back toward the house.

pulling on your sweater eyeing the clock in
the other room   you feel a surge of
adrenaline heat flush come and gone you
look for your leather gloves with less than
10 minutes to go and wonder if you're
catching a cold thin sweat on your back (42
streetcars between 6 and 9)   you feel a
sniffle coming on and breathe in through
your nostrils wet sniffle a drip falls on your
sleeve as you reach for your scarf   you
realize   this is not a cold red wet red
spreading on your sleeve you stride to the
bathroom trying not to get angry as you stuff
some tissue in your nostril and head back to
get your scarf your coat your wallet your
keys   pull the tissue and dampness
springs again head back to the bathroom
to run cold water as you curse the day
curse your nose curse your blood pray for
it to stop grab some tissue as you step out
the door in time to see the streetcar at the
turn   nothing seems to staunch the flow.

pink red cyclamens closing their petals
Georgia O'Keefe whispers blandishments
you have nothing to fear of the storm
whose nervous titters heard from afar
reveal how afraid *it* is.
consider the storm's eye and know
that stillness within motion is the curse
of all flesh. we stretch and pull ourselves along
as if covering distance would unfurl
the road within. prairie grasses brush against
a darkening sky – if you are collapsing know that it is
of your own volition, not the storm around you.

YOUR FLOWERS

I cannot watch you when you arrange the flowers
your pale hands in the window clipping stems
plucking leaves and sinking the buds, one by one
into the the mouth of the vase.

an hour every morning pinching off thorns
you arrange flowers as if practising scales –
with these hands you commemorate music.

roses, irises, gladioli, freesia,
hung upside down in your closet to dry.
if order were the universe
you'd have found heaven by now.

if only the vase were tipped over
the flowers scattered from their arrangement
would your voice from your throat
finally break the air?
                                        like spring
notes in their fledgling psalms
unravelling a brittle harmony.

yesterday's news: a gathering in a church
gutted from years of shelling. no ceiling
or roof cover their scarved heads,
huddled in pews they splay their umbrellas
singing prayers into the tainted rain.

there is someone watching over us
as we gather in public squares and empty corridors,
ritual knotting sense into our lives;
satellites web their way around the earth

and so, we're fed nine seconds from Bosnia
an update, a segment of the past –
and this is what I have of you, a piece
cut off like the tail of a lizard
whose physiognomy knows enough
to preserve itself.

tomorrow I must call a suburb of Sarajevo
and speak with a girl we've interviewed twice on air
to say there's no news on her sponsorship to Canada.
she is the news. she knows this.

I hear crowd clamour from the television set
as I will my hand to pick up the phone.

REUTERS PHOTO

he has brought 5 children onto a clay roof. he is shouting

at someone in front of him, eye-level, as he stands on the peak of his roof

holding 2 little boys by their arms, dangling. 2 little boys

legs mid-air. they wear sneakers.

to the left, on the roof, are 2 other children crying. a girl stands lopsided

holding a sneaker in her hand. she is staring at her father expressionless.

the mother is not in the picture.

the photo shows only the roof, you cannot see the house

you cannot see the neighbouring houses. in the background

concrete hi-rises with balconies.

Man threatens to throw kids off roof in a bid to stop demolition.

it is evening and the children cast long shadows on the roof tiles.

the front door kicked open and doorframe
in splinters, a strong wind *my god*
could suck my things from the foyer
out onto the sidewalk below

blown away. someone's hands
zigzagged through drawers, cracked the CDs
threw knives on the counter, jewelry and
couch cushions scattered on the floor.

the reasoning which held these rooms together
slashed. I leave all lights on and am disarrayed,
wanting to gather my house around me and hide

but there are tracks and the place smells of a
fresh kill. I pace in the kitchen as wind
whips through the hall and out the back door

blindly shutting and opening drawers
my hands shaking helpless, until I realize
it's done. I'm here.
what's gone can be replaced
or be forgotten.

I'm calm now, listening to
gusts of dry leaves
scuttle along the hall,
now that both doors are flapping
I let the outside in.

slump against a doorjamb your soul keening
body leaning, arms folding in. cradled within a
doorway you feel stillness. after earthquakes and
cyclones if anything's standing it's the doorway,
the door itself having been pulled out, hinges
pried apart like fingers.

memory of what was once a threshhold, dwelling,
place of prayer, the doorway divides inside from
out. no one stands there, once you've opened it
you've made half your decision, the door makes
the rest of the decision for you – you walk
through.

but when you pause in a doorway you rest in a
country torn, in the demilitarized zone between
here and there; people pass you.

I stand in doorways with my back against the
jamb looking onto both sides, my body cleaved by
the doorframe, shoulderblades stretching to form wings
to lift this doorframe and all its rooms into
the sky, to turn the world inside out and come
tumbling back down onto a field of green weeds

stay there, on a mountain top in a stone house
with a burnt roof, or walk under an arch into a
room with no ceiling – your eyes opening to blue
sky, you relearn what it means to say you've
entered.

say you turned a corner and sorry forgetting
what you turned away from passed
the red blooms of a hibiscus fluttering with thrushes
heat stilled in your ears. I could shout my love
for you but the world's birds speak more eloquently
than my fingers on you – drops of rain glancing off
an oily green leaf.

say instead you take my hand and hold me steady
for the moment and calm waters cover me
(entering an ocean whose swells have got me
relaxing) a white lighthouse casts a beam
as we plumb the sea for pleasure, passing
the slow stare of a girl seated on a curb
dogs lying on the pavement, ribcages heaving.
as you load the rental car, we turn again passing
bags of cut fruit held up to our windows
pineapple and oranges peeled into halves
mouths split, ready to be eaten.

we drive through the spoils of a land 'always' in summer
with guiltily, gratefully awakened thirst. this fruit
passing from kids' hands to our windows
this fruit passing from my fingers to your lips
take it, take, it is already given.

Now I know, sometimes I was a rooster, sometimes a roe
and these feet turning inward have found swift current
still my hands have seldom seen the sun. only yesterday
maple sap trickled clean from your chest into the smooth
snow around us, we swim with the instincts of tadpoles in a ditch.
I love your wild grass, your smoked thatch, your puddled potholes
now I know I was an antelope, a snail in its shell rolled
the sky peeling autumn leaves and sand up to the knees
an ocean whose salt our bloodstreams breathe. I know
buildings fall, crashing shudders into earth
while in city parking lots trees of heaven find root.
now I know you were an eagle, a mole tunnelling in cool soil
the first spear of aloe on the side of a desert road,
thirst pulling a rusty nail from the hull of a docked boat
wood splinters and knots unloosen, now I know
you are the hand, I am the limb, you are blood
I am skin in this world's uncoiling.

HOUSEWIFE'S TIP #14

take the phone off the hook
after you've booked a ticket to
anywhere.

leave.
don't pack. leave.

3 stones in his pocket won't let him forget
he's heading back to homeland
airplane doors winking shut as a world

folds its hands. close your eyes
fly, find a place to call home
for here is simply too much land
thinly tracked with our landings and crossings.

my house at a crossroads sits above a ravine
filled decades ago with debris. a willow's
roots hooking down to a river I've never seen

there's a green hill that holds my ancestors' bones
like white matchsticks in its closed mouth,
Korea: in this soil even I have a place reserved.

do I fly do I root myself, turn
the map of my skin
out onto a world that fits
(the body folds itself
within another skin)

take my fingers, teeth, my luggage, 2 feet,
with these I can build a foundation

a life, or what passes –
cars, school yards, houses, groceries
fill old riverbeds with mountains until
stone by stone, I uncover them.

NEVER LOOK DOWN IN CHINATOWN

I refuse to smell the garbage as I walk down Chinatown
chicken wings and fish skeletons, soft rotting greens.
early morning garbage trucks come and go, dripping
their stench. you grow used to it
grow blind the way mould spreads quietly
on the underside of fruit.

behind the glass counters at Kim Moon there are
butter buns, coconut buns, winter melon
moon cakes, orange tiles, gold lettering
but in my sinuses, the smell of rotting fruit and meat
(alley kitchen women, their knives and steel basins)

while out front, the sidewalks are relentless.
crowding thick for the morning transactions
we jostle each other, pressing so close
our own faces are lost
in the movement of all people.

Chinatown. somewhere between old world and new
we slipped from the glinting surface, slipped into disguise
and now these market greens, this wickerware
these open crates of fish, these are the national colours.

which part of Asia were you from anyway?
not that it matters, like thronging seagulls
we peck among us and fly off, necks stretched
toward our homes.

there's fish thawing in some young couple's kitchen
23 stories up in a Bay Street condominium
their tap water runs over fish scales and bones,
talismans of a history they've not quite outgrown
things simply grow over.

snow falling white and blanketing everything, it smothers the features of a street, not in layers, but slowly, in particles. like the accumulation of dust, it covers everything becomes weight.

in the dead of winter when you've lived with snow for days and days, you reason it's the same street as always – you know the newspaper box, the graffiti on the corner wall, the fire hydrant with its green ruff of grass.

you forget a street sign was knocked down in a car accident, the graffiti stuccoed over two summers ago, and that branch missing from the ash tree, lost in last fall's storm.

all buried until the thaws come and you forget the snow, forget the storms.

take me to New Orleans in your big broad
boat of a car. I'll sit back with the windows down
bare feet on the dash and toes splayed wide
because of the heat – ain't no other way to drive in Louisiana
land sopping with marshes.

I want to sink into water the way small heads drown
in Manhattan, familiar landmarks recede as
your eye on the horizon
ceases to see. you feel close to
confessing, the tight fingers of your ribs
loosening as centuries are unearthed.
the bog gives up its dead, perfectly preserved
fingers and eyelashes intact.

embalming is the soul's grisly art
of slowing emergencies,
sudden discoveries come unbidden.
so you drive and I'll sink deeper into the seat
you talk and I'll nod but I won't be listening.
just take us to the mangroves whose tangling of roots
breathe life into still waters. there we'll rise
creaky-limbed from the car to finally start moving.

Harrison Ford gazes at photos stacked on his piano
wondering if those pix of his mother are real –
or whose mother is it, do androids long for home?

it wasn't verification he was seeking
but that feeling of having been born into a home
with walls draped in the smells of his mother's cooking,
beds with flannel sheets worn threadbare in that groove
where the body has slumped in its many folds of sleep.

a certain falling together of atoms and incidents
and even on the subway I have felt it.
the train, a safe embassy hurtling me
with godspeed in the tunnels toward home

and dark is the journey we keep falling from
then faltering, we climb back to the Sysiphean dilemma
of what we make our own: the rock, the hill
or the slogging walk of it – is it the place
the loved ones, the rituals?

taking a breather as the rock rolls down again
you survey your house, the trembling cards
about to fall,
by sheer will of decision
they shimmer straight again.

May 12, 3:20 a.m. in a foreign land

this hour of the morning one is so tired
there are no defenses, just unsettledness.
like a leaf lifting on a lawn, nudged by a wind
an unformed need feels its way
within the recess of your ribs.

it is a love waiting to unfold its weight upon the world,
crimson love, heavy as an earlobe on a finger
and as delicate

a world is spawned in one slender moment
sudden skies broadening within my chest
and the particulars of identity become insignificant –
this hand, these cool walls, the rhythm of your breath
the sounds from the street outside our slatted windows,
the sidewalks in Bangkok are not so different.

in this hour, my hand is as simple as any other
as naked as the street beggar's on Ratchaburi Klang
who keeps his head bent down, one palm stretched up.

earlier today, we rushed past such a hand
the man's unheard gesture as quiet as a buddha
observing tourists pass through his temple,
his open palm denudes the world.

this hour of the morning, the earth moves slowly,
one country's night becomes another's day
and I cannot close my eyes.

travelling on the evening train going west
I am saying goodbye to all those I've loved
who are one by one being drawn from my body
into the shallows of a sea.

I was well on my way, but then I lost
the sequence, now I'm caught with
ghosts scrambling onto my shoulders
shouting full-throated avowals –

goodbye I said
left the station long ago.

I am waiting for a still moment
when I and the train have rolled in
and all passengers board and disembark
freely. we arrive together at our destination
no one has to leave.

or perhaps I myself have drifted out
and am waiting for my loved ones to rescue me
as I sit with my eyes fixed on the shore
where the sea merges with land in constant waves.

my close compatriot the leaves are falling
and I don't know where to turn

oh my compatriot the leaves have fallen
and I haven't even asked, have you seen the trees?
as fall comes the leaves brightly burn in our eyes
as fall goes we are left with streets buried in snow

while they fall my friend, the leaves have fallen.
a city come and gone and the rest, they follow
I travel through cities mouthing strange words
seeking a country, a people to name my own
but the leaves are turning and fall has gone,
the sun is setting and I find myself sitting
alone in a barren room.

the leaves fall and have fallen, my compatriot the leaves
turn in the cities turning with the earth, you and I
learn different languages but we mouth the same words.
nations arise in the scaffolds of our minds as our hands
our hands continue their work, building a shifting inheritance.

fall's come and gone and the leaves are still falling,
as streets whiten with sand, here they're buried in snow.
whether I have lived in 12 cities or have hid from the earth
I will ask you this question again in years following
for each time I ask it the leaves have changed,
the sun, the cities, the children have aged
we have aged.

what are the remains
for a people who carry their lifelong possessions
within the fold of their arms?

I must leave a parcel with you.

ANN SHIN
is a Toronto writer and filmmaker.